W9-AUE-077

SPOTLIGHT ON
IMMIGRATION AND MIGRATION

THE DREAM OF MANIFEST DESTINY

IMMIGRANTS AND THE WESTWARD EXPANSION

Nick Christopher

PowerKiDS press.

NEW YORK

Published in 2016 by The Rosen Publishing Group, Inc.
29 East 21st Street, New York, NY 10010

Copyright © 2016 by The Rosen Publishing Group, Inc.

All rights reserved. No part of this book may be reproduced in any form without permission
in writing from the publisher, except by a reviewer.

Editor: Katie Kawa
Book Design: Samantha DeMartin / Laura Bowen

Photo Credits: Cover Slick-o-bot/Wikimedia Commons; pp. 4, 19 MPI/Archive Photos/Getty Images;
p. 5 Fotosearch/Archive Photos/Getty Images; p. 7 Calliopejen1/Wikimedia Commons; pp. 8 (both), 16,
17, 21, 22 Everett Historical/Shutterstock.com; p. 9 SuperStock/Getty Images; p. 10 Universal History Archive/
Universal Images Group Editorial/Getty Images; p. 11 John Parrot/Stocktrek Images/Getty Images; pp. 12-13
Mike Nelson/AFP/Getty Images; pp. 14-15 Durova/Wikimedia Commons; p. 18 American Stock Archive/Archive
Photos/Getty Images; p. 20 File Upload Bot (Magnus Manske)/Wikimedia Commons.

Library of Congress Cataloging-in-Publication Data

Christopher, Nick.
The dream of Manifest Destiny : immigrants and the westward expansion / Nick Christopher.
    pages cm. — (Spotlight on immigration and migration)
 Includes index.
ISBN 978-1-5081-4071-9 (pbk.)
ISBN 978-1-5081-4072-6 (6 pack)
ISBN 978-1-5081-4074-0 (library binding)
1. Manifest Destiny. 2. United States—Territorial expansion—Juvenile literature. 3. West (U.S.)—Discovery and
exploration—Juvenile literature. 4. West (U.S.)—History—19th century—Juvenile literature. I. Title.
E179.5.C45 2016
978'.02—dc23
                                    2015023454

Manufactured in the United States of America

CPSIA Compliance Information: Batch #BW16PK: For further information contact Rosen Publishing, New York, New York at 1-800-237-9932.

CONTENTS

A LAND OF OPPORTUNITY

People from all over Europe began to settle in North America during the 1600s. The French, Spanish, and British were among the first people to sail westward across the Atlantic Ocean to establish **permanent** settlements in what they called the New World.

By the 1700s, the British had established 13 colonies along the eastern coast of what's now the United States. In 1776, the British colonists declared their independence from their mother country and formed their own nation.

After America gained its independence, more land was opened to settlers for exploration. The West began to interest **immigrants** and those whose families had been living in America since colonial times. They saw the West as a land of opportunity in the same way those first European immigrants saw North America as a place to find wealth and a fresh start.

"Manifest **Destiny**" was a phrase used to describe Americans' belief that it was their destiny to expand the country until it reached from the Atlantic Ocean to the Pacific Ocean.

GAINING WESTERN LANDS

In the years following the **American Revolution**, interest in westward expansion began to increase. However, there were **obstacles** for Americans to overcome before they could claim land in the West. France and Mexico already owned large areas of western territory.

In 1803, President Thomas Jefferson bought the French-owned Louisiana Territory for $15 million. This is known as the Louisiana Purchase. The land **stretched** from the Mississippi River to the Rocky Mountains. Mexico owned land that stretched west of Louisiana to the Pacific Ocean. After fighting a war with Mexico that lasted from 1846 to 1848, the United States gained even more land in the West. These lands included the areas that would become all or part of the states of Texas, California, New Mexico, Arizona, Colorado, Nevada, Utah, and Wyoming. People soon began to **migrate** to these new lands in the West from other parts of the country.

The Treaty of Guadalupe Hidalgo officially ended the Mexican-American War. This treaty gave the United States more western lands, which extended the boundaries of the country to the Pacific Ocean. With the signing of this treaty, the dream of Manifest Destiny was realized.

EXPLORING THE WEST

After the Louisiana Purchase was completed in 1803, Jefferson sent a group of explorers on a journey through the new lands the United States had acquired. Jefferson was hoping this expedition would discover a water route that connected the United States to the Pacific Ocean. Jefferson also wanted to establish trade with Native Americans in these new lands.

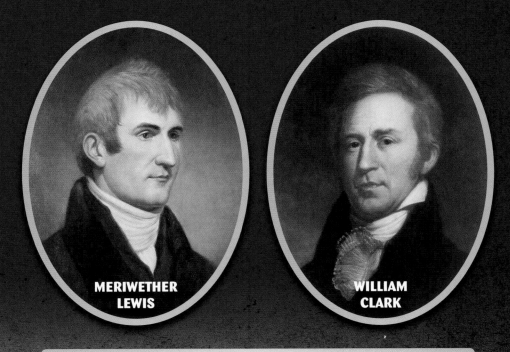

MERIWETHER LEWIS

WILLIAM CLARK

Jefferson's personal secretary, Meriwether Lewis, was one of the leaders of this expedition. The other was William Clark. They set off on May 14, 1804, from St. Louis, Missouri. Lewis and Clark left with a small group known as the Corps of Discovery. Their journey to the Pacific Ocean and back took over two years. They returned to St. Louis on September 23, 1806.

Lewis and Clark met with many Native Americans during their journey. They believed it was their job to tell Native Americans they were now living on land owned by the United States.

IMPACT ON NATIVE AMERICANS

Westward expansion in North America had a big impact on the lives of Native Americans living in western lands. When the first European immigrants came to North America, there were millions of Native Americans living all over the continent. The immigrants wanted Native Americans to leave their homelands, and sometimes this led to **violence**.

As settlers began to travel west, they often fought with the Native Americans who had been living in North America long before Europeans arrived. Over the years, this fighting resulted in losses on both sides. However, the Native American population was hit the hardest by these battles. By the end of the 1800s, most Native Americans had been forced to migrate to reservations, which were pieces of land set aside for them by the U.S. government.

The biggest victory for the Native Americans in the West was the Battle of the Little Bighorn in 1876. However, it was also the last big victory they would have against settlers and the U.S. military.

11

THE MORMONS MOVE TO UTAH

Some people who traveled to the West did so for religious reasons. The Mormons were one religious group that migrated to the West. The Mormon Church was founded in New York State by Joseph Smith in 1830. Many people disagreed with the

beliefs of Mormons and **persecuted** them. After Smith was killed, most Mormons headed west to look for a new place to safely and freely practice their religion.

This Mormon migration was led by Brigham Young. The Mormons traveled west in covered wagons and on foot along what became known as the Mormon Trail. Between 1846 and 1869, about 70,000 Mormons moved to Utah. Utah is still the center of the Mormon religion, and people travel there to this day to practice Mormon beliefs.

Shown here is a modern reenactment of Mormons traveling by covered wagon along the Mormon Trail.

GOLD!

The discovery of gold changed the West—especially California—in a major way. Gold was first discovered in 1848 on the American River in California. This discovery started the California gold rush. Word of this discovery quickly spread, and soon the area was flooded with people from every corner of the world.

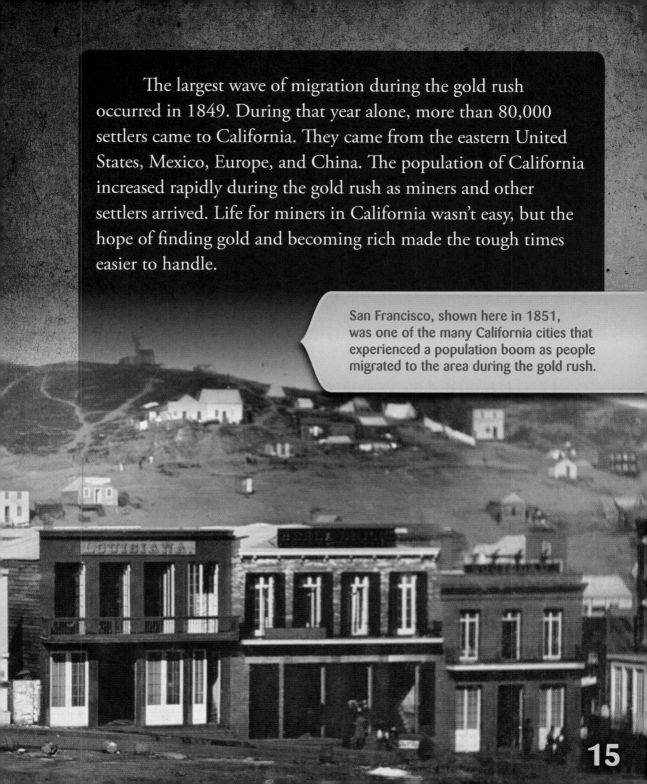

The largest wave of migration during the gold rush occurred in 1849. During that year alone, more than 80,000 settlers came to California. They came from the eastern United States, Mexico, Europe, and China. The population of California increased rapidly during the gold rush as miners and other settlers arrived. Life for miners in California wasn't easy, but the hope of finding gold and becoming rich made the tough times easier to handle.

San Francisco, shown here in 1851, was one of the many California cities that experienced a population boom as people migrated to the area during the gold rush.

LIFE ON A HOMESTEAD

The U.S. government wanted to make sure all the new lands it acquired in the West were settled. In 1862, President Abraham Lincoln signed the Homestead Act, which was meant to encourage the migration of U.S. citizens to the West. The government feared that if lands in the West were left unoccupied, they would be taken by Mexican gangs or by the **displaced** Native Americans.

The Homestead Act allowed citizens to settle on 160 acres (64.7 ha) of unclaimed public land in the West for free. In return, the settlers would work on the land and make improvements. After five years, the settlers would officially own the land. Many settlers migrated west because of the Homestead Act.

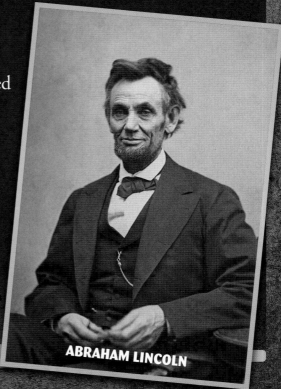

ABRAHAM LINCOLN

Whole families, such as the one shown in this 1886 photograph, moved west because of the Homestead Act.

WESTWARD IN WAGONS

Hundreds of thousands of immigrants came to the West between 1840 and 1870 looking for new opportunities and a fresh start. They came from places as far away as China and Russia. People also migrated to the West from the eastern parts of the United States in large numbers.

Early migrating families, called pioneers, traveled in covered wagons pulled by oxen or mules. They stayed together in wagon trains because they felt safer in groups. One wagon train could consist of anywhere from 30 to 100 wagons. Most trains traveled between 12 and 20 miles (19.3 and 32.2 km) per day. The journey wasn't easy, but the people who traveled in wagon trains believed they were heading toward a better life in the West.

Wagon trains traveled on all the main trails that connected the eastern and western areas of the United States, including the Mormon Trail and the **Oregon Trail**, shown here.

THE TRANSCONTINENTAL RAILROAD

Railroads completely changed the way people traveled west. In 1862, Congress passed the first Pacific Railway Act. Two railroad companies were commissioned to build a railroad that would run from Nebraska to California, meeting somewhere in the middle. This would be the last link in creating a transcontinental railroad, or a railroad that ran across the continent of North America.

A golden spike was hammered into the ground to mark the completion of the transcontinental railroad. Many immigrants helped make the dream of a transcontinental railroad a reality.

The railroad companies found they had a lack of workers. They hired many Chinese immigrants who settled in the West. At first, no one believed these immigrants were strong enough to do the job. However, they skillfully dug tunnels and flattened rock with **dynamite**. On May 10, 1869, the two railroads met in Utah. Many people gathered to celebrate the completion of the first transcontinental railroad.

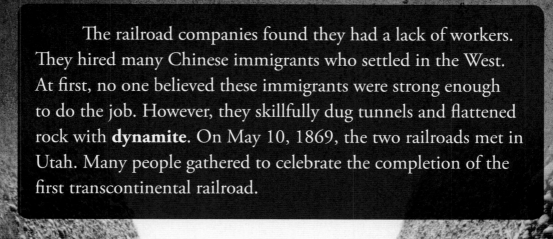

Dynamite blasted through rock to create the Central Pacific Railroad's Bloomer Cut, which is shown here.

MANIFEST DESTINY

The history of westward expansion in the United States is filled with stories of action, adventure, and danger. In 1845, a political writer named John L. O'Sullivan was the first person to call Americans' desire to move westward Manifest Destiny. However, he was certainly not the last to use this term to describe the push to expand America westward.

The fulfillment of the idea of Manifest Destiny started with Lewis and Clark's expedition in 1804. They told the Native Americans they met that the United States now owned their western lands. By 1849, the United States reached "from sea to shining sea." Westward migration led to Manifest Destiny becoming a reality less than 100 years after the American Revolution.

GLOSSARY

American Revolution: A war that lasted from 1775 to 1783 in which the American colonists won independence from British rule.

destiny: The events that will necessarily happen to a person or thing in the future.

displace: To force people to leave the area where they live.

dynamite: A powerful explosive often used in the form of a stick.

immigrant: A person who comes to a country to live there.

migrate: To move from one place to settle in another.

obstacle: Something that stops forward movement or progress.

Oregon Trail: A land route that ran from Independence, Missouri, to Oregon Territory.

permanent: Lasting for a very long time or forever.

persecute: To treat a person or group of people cruelly or unfairly, especially because of race or religious or political beliefs.

stretch: To become extended.

violence: The use of physical force in a way meant to harm someone.

INDEX

PRIMARY SOURCE LIST

Cover. *Westward the Course of Empire Takes Its Way.* Created by Emanuel Gottlieb Leutze. 1861. Oil on canvas. Now kept at the Smithsonian American Art Museum, Washington, D.C.

Page 5. *American Progress.* Print, based on original created by John Gast. 1872. Original now kept at the Museum of the American West, Los Angeles, California.

Page 10. *What's Left of Big Foot's Band.* Created by John C. H. Grabill. 1891. Photograph.

Page 14. Portsmouth Square, San Francisco, California. Created by Sterling C. McIntyre. January 1851. Photograph (daguerreotype). Now kept at the Library of Congress Prints and Photographs Division, Washington, D.C.

WEBSITES

Due to the changing nature of Internet links, PowerKids Press has developed an online list of websites related to the subject of this book. This site is updated regularly. Please use this link to access the list: www.powerkidslinks.com/soim/westex